A Guide to CHANGE

When Your Family Has a Baby

Written by
E.C. Andrews

KidHaven
PUBLISHING

Published in 2026 by
KidHaven Publishing, an Imprint of
Greenhaven Publishing, LLC
2544 Clinton St., Buffalo, NY 14224

Written by: E.C. Andrews
Edited by: Rebecca Phillips-Bartlett
Designed by: Amelia Harris

Cataloging-in-Publication Data
Names: Andrews, E.C.
Title: When your family has a baby / E.C. Andrews.
Description: Buffalo, NY : Kidhaven Publishing, 2026. | Series: A Guide to Change | Includes glossary and index
Identifiers: ISBN 9781534550186 (pbk) | ISBN 9781534550193 (library bound) | ISBN 9781534550209 (ebook)
Subjects: LCSH: Adoption—Juvenile Literature | Pregnancy—Juvenile Literature | Siblings—Juvenile Literature
Classification: LCC BF723.S43 A53 2026 | DDC 155.44/3--dc25

Manufactured in the United States of America

CPSIA compliance information: Batch #CSKH26
For further information contact Greenhaven Publishing LLC at 1-844-317-7404.

Please visit our website, www.greenhavenpublishing.com.
For a free color catalog of all our high-quality books, call toll free 1-844-317-7404 or fax 1-844-317-7405.

Find us on

Image Credits

All images are courtesy of Shutterstock.com, unless otherwise stated. Cover – Monkey Business Images, TobinCStudio, Zakharchenko Anna. Recurring – Alenka Karabanova, RidiUmbrella. 4–5 – myboys.me, Pikovit, alinabuphoto, PeopleImages.com - Yuri A. 6–7 – FamVeld, Bricolage. 8–9 Krakenimages.com, Monkey Business Images. 10–11 – fizkes, Iryna Dincer. 12–13 – polkadot_photo, wavebreakmedia, CuteDesigns. 14–15 – PeopleImages.com - Yuri A, Monkey Business Images, YummyBuum. 16–17 – pikselstock, Dollydoll29. 18–19 – Pavel L Photo and Video, Prostock-studio, Chipolla. 20–21 – privilege, Antonio Guillem. 22–23 – Monkey Business Images, MIA Studio.

Contents

WORDS THAT LOOK LIKE THIS CAN BE FOUND IN THE GLOSSARY ON PAGE 24.

Change Is All Around Us

Change is always happening around us. Day changes to night. The weather outside changes over time. You probably change your socks every day. You may change which toys you play with or what you eat for lunch.

Some changes happen without us noticing. Other changes can have a big impact on our lives. Big changes can cause big feelings. These changes can be exciting. However, they can also make you feel worried.

GOING TO A NEW SCHOOL IS A BIG CHANGE.

MOVING CAN BE A VERY EXCITING CHANGE.

When Your Family Has a Baby

If your family has a new baby, you will be inviting a new person into the family. That is a big change! If your parent is having a baby, they will be your new younger brother or sister.

A BROTHER OR SISTER IS CALLED A SIBLING.

There are different ways a family can have a new baby. Your parent may spend nine months growing the baby in their body. This is called pregnancy. Your family could also adopt a baby or use a surrogate.

IF YOUR FAMILY USES A SURROGATE OR ADOPTS, NO ONE AT HOME WILL BE PREGNANT.

Why Do I Feel This Way?

Having a new sibling can be very exciting. However, you may find yourself feeling worried or upset. It is OK if you feel this way. It is normal to have big feelings when change happens.

You may feel worried about changes in the house or about your family member going to the hospital if they are pregnant. It may feel upsetting seeing your family spending lots of time with the new baby.

FEELING UPSET WHEN SOMEONE HAS SOMETHING YOU WANT IS SOMETIMES CALLED JEALOUSY.

Think About Your Feelings

It is OK to feel a mixture of feelings when your family is welcoming a new baby. You may feel excited and worried at the same time. This may feel confusing.

Allow yourself to feel your emotions. When you start having big feelings, try asking yourself some check-in questions.

Talk About Your Feelings

Remember that it is normal to feel lots of different emotions when big changes happen. Whatever you are feeling, talking about it can help you make sense of it.

Try talking to a trusted grown-up about your feelings. Find a quiet place where you will not be interrupted. Be honest about how you feel. This will make it easier for the grown-up to help.

Read and Learn

Knowing more about what to expect can help you feel less worried. Ask your family questions about the new baby and how they will arrive. There is no such thing as a silly question.

Try reading some books about being an older sibling. Learn how things will change as you both get older. Once you know what to expect, you can learn ways to help take care of your sibling.

Coping with Change

Your family will need to spend more time with the new baby. This is because the baby will need help with a lot of things that big kids can do by themselves.

YOUR FAMILY WILL LOVE YOU JUST AS MUCH AS THE NEW BABY.

You are very important to your new sibling. Help your family find ways of making your new sibling feel welcome. Although this change can feel hard, getting involved before the baby comes can help this change feel better.

Getting Ready

Getting ready for your new sibling to arrive can be a very exciting process. Try picking out some toys you think they might like or help your family get your new sibling's bedroom ready.

HOW ELSE COULD YOU HELP TO WELCOME YOUR NEW SIBLING?

If your family member is having the baby, they often have to go to the hospital to give birth. This may seem scary. Ask your family member about their hospital stay. Try helping them pack their things.

PEOPLE GIVE BIRTH IN A HOSPITAL SO DOCTORS CAN CARE FOR THEM.

Welcoming the New Baby

When your new sibling arrives, you will be able to meet them for the first time. This may mean going to the hospital. Or your family member may bring your sibling home for you to meet them.

Try preparing a special welcome gift for your sibling. This could be something you have made such as a letter or a picture. Some people give soft toys or special ornaments for a new baby.

ASK A GROWN-UP TO HELP YOU PICK OUT A GIFT.

Embracing Change

As your sibling settles in, start spending time with them. Learn about things you can safely help them with. Try talking to them or singing songs with them. Help them get to know you.

ASK A GROWN-UP FAMILY MEMBER FOR HELP IF YOU WANT TO HOLD THE BABY.

Getting a new sibling is a big change. You may be feeling many things. However, it can be very exciting. After all, a new sibling can be a friend for life.

TALK TO GROWN-UPS ABOUT YOUR FEELINGS AS OFTEN AS YOU NEED TO.

Glossary

adopt	to legally make a baby or child part of a family they were not born into
ornaments	items that can hang on a Christmas tree
surrogate	a person who grows a baby in their body for other people who want to be parents
trusted	believed to be truthful, honest, and reliable

Index